The Seasoned Woman

I0620474

Praise for *The Seasoned Woman*

The Seasoned Woman creates a cascade of images as brilliant as star points, sends emotions swirling through the mind that land hushed as dew in the heart. I am inspired by Andrea Vocab Sanderson.

USA Today best-selling author Laura Castoro

The words of Sanderson travel through my mind, my heart and my spirit like a raging river, opening out into the sea. Taking us through the streets and stories of women, aging, young, braving and in the heavens, Sanderson's *The Seasoned Woman* is a sultry and delicious invitation to experience the divine feminine as she powers and flows with the changing rhythms of time.

Anel I.Flores, author of **Curtains of Rain** *and* **Empanada: A Lesbiana Story en Probaditas**

Earth Mother, Vocab, explores the divine feminine in these poetic verses and lyric psalms reminding us of the divine which is always present in each of us and that every second is sacred.

American Book Award winner Amalia Ortiz

Andrea "Vocab" Sanderson is a force of nature. *The Seasoned Woman* is a soulful dance of deep contemplation, witness, and wonder through the changing seasons of womanhood. These lyrical poems are song, prayer, and salve.

Amanda Johnston, 2024 Texas Poet Laureate

The Seasoned Woman
Copyright © 2025 Andrea Sanderson

Cover Art by Miguel Mauras

The font used is Georgia

All rights reserved. No duplication or reuse of any selection is allowed without the express written consent of the publisher.

Gnashing Teeth Publishing
242 East Main Street
Norman AR 71960
http://GnashingTeethPublishing.com

Printed in the United States of America

ISBN 978-1-966075-02-8

Non-Fiction: Poetry

Gnashing Teeth Publishing First Edition

We carve monuments to men like the peaks of Rushmore, but what about the women who move mountains?

Andrea "VOCAB" Sanderson

Table of Contents

Foreword

The Seasoned Woman, by Andrea Vocab Sanderson, is a testament to time and the turn of the seasons in an unforgiving world where the sacredness of the human body is often forgotten and reduced to a desperate battle with creams and crows' feet, beauty a fugitive running in desperation and the holiness of the "temple carved out of spirit and bones" not reverenced. Such poetic songs of exaltation and resistance as "The Body as Religion" and "Sacred Tongues" evoke the power of "relishing the resplendence of our form", this body-place "enthroned with awe-inspiring wonders." The inherent feminism in this celebration of physicality, of the female body, of the diversity of female lives of significance, and of passion "where the peace and pieces of God rest upon our skin" inspires us to respect the heat of love, to "set the sanctuary on fire", and to revere the "words so sacred I cannot pronounce." The only thing better than reading these poems, is to hear them in Sanderson's own melodically passionate voice. *The Seasoned Woman* is a gem, and leaves us all standing taller and prouder and more solidly encamped in the sacred temples of our own bodies.

Carmen Tafolla, State Poet Laureate of Texas 2015

(R)evolutions of Womanhood

Solstice to equinox, we never cease, we rarely stop
Greening with youthfulness to ripened with age
Bittersweet nectars dripping onto the pages of life
We span and spin
Orbiting the sun in these layers of skin

Crystals of sea salt to coarsely ground peppercorn
Watch it wilt and be reborn time and time again
Freshly plucked and pruned
The harvesting of crescent moons
The cutting of umbilical cord from the bellies of our personal galaxy
We recognize purging is as necessary a process as
digging, planting, and watering.
We realize some woman, somewhere
is giving birth to something
at all times.

Our doulas prepare with cupped palms for
 the catching and midwife receiving.
In sisterhood, we readily await, present in heart and mind.
Holding hands, we press through the travail of a process
to help her manifest it all.
We build upon breath and stretch the body
 through fall, winter, spring, and summer
a number of revolutions,
a tumult of time tumbling,
a progression of nightshades and berries on the vine.
Amongst thorns and veiny growth we flourish and
wither as the seasons whisper,
howl, and sing.

Autumn Leaves (Redux)

Drift, flutter, spin to the pavement
Drop, descend, saunter to the soil
Sink, dip, shimmy to the earth
In clusters shake, float, fall

This is the season of all deteriorating.
The echoed call of collapsing towers.
The leaves perform a ballet of decay in the air around us.
The casualties and rubble of war wilting like the evidence of autumn
Surround us surmounting with the reverberation of
Crisp, crackle, crunch. Break!
A cornucopia of sound escaping beneath our feet, and I know,
The branches miss their faithful family
How they must ache and rustle in distress
Bend to the moist but barren dirt longing to gather them again.
I cannot pretend that my limbs do not feel the same dark mourning.

The bark, forlorn for the stark space at the end of empty fingertips.
The place once occupied by the green foliage of friendship.
Imagining: kinship, closeness, and utterances returned.
Now, I'm spurning in silence, learning to embrace
The recollection of experiences,
Before the violence that begat my solitude.
I will not chat with apparitions, although wishful for your words.
As I yearn for the fallen,
I will observe the interludes, brief and elongated
Recanting only in my memory –

As I shudder and grieve, amongst the collage of red and golden
leaves.

In-between The Seasons

I sit in this moment, perplexed. Questioning everything about
      myself: stability, vulnerability, and the access of villainous
      disappointments.
I sit befuddled with my feuding thoughts battling each other.
Conquered with agony and regret as my adversaries. Unsure of my
      next direction. I can only pace in place. And I would hate to
      move forward without clarity in view.
Is it the right time to do something new? (Is it the right time?)
I sit avoiding mirrors. Reliving memories. Ruminating. Ashamed.
Cud lodged in the molars of my rotating mouth, trying to spit
      something out. Decipher through doubt. Where did I get this
      wrong? Things that I thought I knew all along. My
      meditations, a replayed song, no skips, just repeats. Feeling
      stuck in a dungeon of defeats. Contemplating what really
      brings me happiness. How do I define success?
What will the rest of my days look like if I cannot manifest the
      continuation of a failed plan? I lament, I lament; and I
      struggle to understand.

With no spring in my step, no heated press of summer, no harvest
      of fall, no turning of winter to ice.

With no spring in my step, no heated press of summer, no harvest
      of fall, no turning of winter to ice.

With no spring in my step, no heated press of summer, no harvest
      of fall, no turning of winter to ice.

Two Pink Shoes

I am smitten tonight, bitten by fright, folding my heart under
fluorescent light. Incessant rattling and a fight before
midnight, because this one came in drunk. The officers said s
he stunk the funk of no showers and desolation. Prostitution
her means of preservation destination unknown.
She ran away from home intoxicated by the cologne of death and
destruction. Functioning marginally, fifteen, pregnant, and
HIV positive doing whatever she can to live. Diabetic and
sick as an infirmary with nothing to give the world, but grief. All
alone, I only hear suffering when she speaks. Her shoes are
pink. They lay prostrate under door number eight as she
waits for processing. You see, I work the third shift at
Juvenile Detention Center. Every time I enter that building, I
get the distinct feeling of childhood burdens peeling away the
weightlessness of my personal life.
I thought I knew strife and hard times, until I saw these teenagers
facing hard time for the crimes of delinquency. The
frequency of their screams disturbs my dreams, but I cannot
nod off on my shift, responding to routine checks as officers
inspect rooms one by one. Our job isn't done until someone
comes to relieve us. So I just sit all night, fight the sleep that
astounds me, search the silence around me, trying to not feel
as caged and enraged as the youths we supervise.
Mostly the girls cry, the boys seldom do, but the agony and
desperation in their faces always holds true. You've never
seen hopelessness, until it is reflected through the soul of a
child. You've never seen ruthlessness and tragedy gone wild,
until you've seen the faces attached to the files on these
hardship cases. And while I sit in Main Control, and Juvenile
Officers patrol, and I see soles stack up two by two.
I want to take these shoes and throw them back in the face of every

dilemma that brought them here. This Center is like a Noah's Ark of dejection and fear. Herding them in two by two. We try to provide protection from the storm outside. But sometimes we merely help them survive. Is there really safety inside when their minds torture them with guilt and circumstance? Rehabilitation is a luxury. Can they be afforded a second chance?

Some do a dance with fate, like the girl sitting behind door number eight, inflating demon's egos fate just stepped on her toes. Her future will be lethal, like the HIV that she passes to her unborn. Those pink shoes know the scorn of innocence torn.

She just: sits, and waits, mourns and suffers, and I can't help but wonder: will she finally drown when she is released from this ark without us to cover her—from the rain and pain that stains those two pink shoes.

She Spoke of Wounds

She spoke a century of injuries from her wounded mouth, her words
tied us in a tight tourniquet to cauterize the spilling blood.
And in all of this perilous speaking the space is marked, drawn in
the sands.
We shall courageously embark to reclaim the land.
Our voices lift as steam from an oasis with a liberating boldness
that defies, telling a portrait worth a million wounds.

The abrasions of conquest and violence are numerous worldwide.
People of Ukraine, Yemen, Sudan, Syria, Somalia, Afghanistan,
Iraq, Palestine, Congo, Libya and even more: she called to you
and you.
Lamented for the mass exodus of Congolese escaping to Goma in
desperation fleeing the M23.
Offered a soft soliloquy for the over 13 million starving Yemeni
people.

She let out a litany for the border-crossings of Rafah to Erez, the
double-crossing of Palestinian people, Gaza cut across the
throat with genocide.
Precious people knocked to the dirt, are gathering from gardens of
stony debris.
From script and scroll, they ascend in a crescendo of resistance
against offense, stigmatized as cycling in a constant state of
conflict.

She sought a salve in her words to end the rotation.

She recanted an accurate adaptation revealing the history of
struggle: where thieving hands tug at the resources of
domestic or foreign lands to gain access to political power

time and time again. Civil wars are incited by alleged allies to disrupt sound structures, until civilians rise and take a stand.

She told of broken resolutions, treaties, and disrupted vows. She foretold the attempted discontinuation of nations, fractured by factions.

She made a verbal petition of action against the rivalries. Then alliances were formed for campaigns of uprising.

The expository sheds light on the true story:
In a sackcloth of mourning we bow our heads.
Beauty for ashes, as to flowers for the dead.
A chorus of voices cry at the dirge. Bearing witness to women and men stripped of their dignity, young people dying and surviving from the violation of their bodies, and children forcefully abducted from their families.
Human beings constricted in regions polluted by toxic refuse and the clouds cast by the smoky aftermath of bomb blasts are often the last to be rescued, spoken of, or sought.

She says you are not an afterthought, nor are you forgotten.
She utters for each one of your battered bodies a faith-filled prayer.
She bravely chants *cease fire now*
She proclaims a passionate protest for equitable justice, and a celestial supplication of peace.

The Body As Religion

We grieve the absence of youth savoring sacraments of nostalgic
    seconds. We spend the best parts of our lives seeking Sankofa
    and reclaiming the fragmented parts of our nature. We desire
    the nurture of our heart and soul to let our body language
    fluidly speak with zeal. Revealing a motif of movement suited to
    our Sacred, yes our Sacred.

That we may testify of it a space, whether it: sanctuary, synagogue,
    shrine or mosque, your flesh is simply a temple carved out of
    spirit and bones. A place enthroned with awe inspiring wonders
    from sharpened shoulder blades to thighs that thunder. We
    shall humbly exalt the vessel we've been given.

We are no longer compelled and driven by outside force or coerced
    into relishing the resplendence of our form. We willingly
    perform the ceremony of self-love daily. Holding space for the
    beauty bestowed in our bosoms. With rituals of rites day and
    night we fight to preserve and let go of the things that no longer
    serve our inner majesty.

This is the physical place where the peace and pieces of God rest upon
    our skin, from the scalp of our crowning glory to the pedestal of
    our twinkling toes. For the freckles, birthmarks, and moles, for
    the wrinkles, scars of demarcation, and crows that flock in the
    folds of our face. Cherish the intricate altars built-up, burnt
    down, and replaced by the residual and individual seconds
    spreading across your skin. We need to see the gathered
    moments of our timeline as a blessing, not vexed.
Dripping with oil. We face the turmoil of aging. We will reap the spoils
    for it is our keepsake at the highest stakes to divinely delight in
    at our discretion. The body as religion.

Lila's Enchantment

Lila May Cockrell fell in love with the San Antonio River while strolling with her husband Sidney Earl along a downtown sidewalk. Bemused by the Mariachi and colorful culture of a major city bustling with delight, this petite brunette found A *Love Deeper Than the River,* and it became a reflection of her strength.

The first female mayor of our city served consecutive terms, 1975-81 and 1989-91. She yearned to give back to a budding metropolis that was Hemisfair and so refined. Fully aware of her call to action she summoned the strength to lead us, with a slew of firsts lined under her belt. First Councilwoman of San Antonio, 1963. First woman President of Texas Municipal League. She rode the WAVES of the seven seas with service to the Navy, WAVES an acronym for: Women Accepted Volunteer Emergency Service. We herald her for the jewel she was and is. Environmentalist, we benefit from her indelible blueprint across the entire Lone Star state. Emeritus, we honor her for the leadership she implemented to set the River City apart from the rest. Empress, Lila, you said you were enchanted by the city. The sweet sorcery of our traditions touching the cornerstone of your skin. The wonder of our heartbeat pounding beneath your chest. You let the passion for the Missions fuel you to conserve and preserve all of the precious magic of the land where we stand. Then you, yourself, cast a grand spell over San Antonio and it hasn't been broken since.

RAP: Spanning Space

She is Enraptured in the dance
That girl's Compelling every glance
The Instrumental guides
The glory in her strides
Her hips flow & slide
Body rolls, glows & glides
Swaying like the tides
tempo derived from the deep soul inside
Like a new ragtime, liwa, or baladi
The Ghawazi Spanning space
 satin soft in every place
Controlling her bo-dy with hypnotic me-lo-dy
Hear the cluck of mother tongue
Su-mmon(ing) seasoned & young
Language in the femme form
Spin the space like a storm
Diasporas reborn.
Diasporas reborn!
Lamma Bada yah!

Summer Seasoning

A blended spice scorching my taste for any other season. Summer, you
   came in hot like cayenne. Rested on the tip of my tongue. I
   couldn't play coy with you. Heat meeting my lips. You turned
   my temperature torrid!
I was reeling from the way you roasted me, radiating from your waves.
Tingles, throbbing and thrilling, but never leaving me numb.

You dare me to be brave. The burning increased in the crevasses of my
   body. We baked easy, basting in a rotation like a succulent
   rotisserie.
With you came the release of sweat and inhibitions. Summer always
   turning my ignition, awakening forgotten ambitions.
 I was turned on and a new me was born. Begging to be brazen.
   Begging to bang any coldness right out of the sky. No clouds to
   block your hovering heat.
Summer it was you and I!

With no reservations you melted into my life: a rumbling party of one,
   ready for fun.
I say you set this sanctuary on fire. Ghost peppers gripping your girth
   and width, savagely ripping with rage on these solstice days.
   Emancipating my palate. Summer, you simmered a titan in the
   skyline. COURAGEOUS CAJUN FLAVOR came boundless in.
   Ample, resting a whole heap of hotness right on my skin. One
   minute I was chewing, the next minute I was choking.
   Intolerable temperatures ruptured the atmosphere. It's too hot
   in here!! I am used to fear on my palate. But now only freedom
   is bubbling blood pressure high. And only I understand why I
   am bravely burning.

It's Summertime and supremacy is like a speakeasy. Say the magic
word and suddenly you've gained access to an exclusive
seclusion, a well painted illusion, a Great Gatsby of good ole boy
intoxication. A place where oppression has never really left or
lifted its' foot off of the neck of the 99%. We are jumping back
into the high cotton of racism and sexism! Every time the
Supreme Court, or a governor, or a president overturns
legislation, I am reminded of, The Birth of a Nation. Where the
only way to save us is for the Klansmen to come rolling in and
restore all of the values that made America so, so great, in the
first place. One of these mornings you're gonna rise up singing
and you won't even recognize the oppression, I mean
progression of the sharp turn to conservatism of the last sixty
years. So hush little baby no more tears or night terrors. This is
a century of trial by blunders and errors, warfare, and bloody
despair that can be quietly repaired by the time you come of
age.

We will rewrite history's pages with a more pleasant font so speak
naught, and
don't
don't
don't
you cry.

Sisterhood Summertime (Remix)

Here it is. The groove is slightly transformed.
They've made a drastic change to political norms.
Progress reversed feels like the end of democracy.
A hard-core war on womanhood
 it's gotten to be a little bit outta control.
High time we redesign antiquated gender roles.
Add liberation to the equation.
Raise fists and resist.
We gotta & vote to fix it!

We can't relive the summers of the past.
Sisters stand up. Let this anthem blast.
Lubana singin' out. Vocab run a rhyme.
It's your choice. Lift your voice (oh yeah)
Cuz this summertime

Chorus:
Summer, summer, summertime.
Sisterhood is on my mind.

Summer, summer, summertime.
Sisterhood is on my mind.
Sisterhood is on mind.
Summer, summer, summertime.
Sisterhood is on my mind.

Verse 2:

Women's Rights. Yeah, it's kind of a buzz.
Solidarity and unity, a movement of love.
Repping sisters as allies, major problems exist.

Shift the culture with redefinition of "summer mad-ness."
We got to be aggressive, patriarchy is oppressive.
Activism with wisdom. Stand-up be & expressive.
Can't avoid the issues or the misuse of power.
Sistershood is strong in this song. We're not cowards.
Empowered to devour the systems & setbacks.
Together- weather - seasons of lack.
Resource sharing and caring for community,
Body positivity, alleviating scrutiny.
Plenty of heavy issues were on my mind.
I remixed Will Smith with these seasoned lines.
With a phone & iPad I composed this rhyme.
To hype you up & get you equipped for the Summertime.

Chorus:
Summer, summer, summertime.
Sisterhood is on my mind.

Summer, summer, summertime.
Sisterhood is on my mind.
Sisterhood is on my mind.
Summer, summer, summertime.
Sisterhood is on my mind.

The rainy nights of September remind me of your eyes.

I hope the winds, if you forget me and do not return,
Are forgotten too by the clouds and the moon,
And its nights grow longer,
And we become strangers, September and I.

Rest

Repose for the soul sounds like silence in the garden
Being planted in serenity allowing for reflection and growth.
Looks like transit to fertile terrains
Remaining in the presence of nutrients and nurturing hands.
Gaining ground as we get back up on our feet again.

We aren't pushing these petals to bloom too soon.
We are experiencing the process
Digressing and believing the manifestation will happen
in tune with God's timing

Until then, I am aligning myself with peace and living unstressed.
For the burden of being overworked does not mean I am
Blessed with opportunity. Having ourselves overwhelmed by
        circumstance is not a gift.
We can cultivate our soil better after we've rested in our skin.
Sometimes we need to marinate on our mantras, meditate on where
        we've been, as well as where we're going. Yes doing all of this
        from the perspective of a dream state.
Spirit can speak clarity in your dreams.
 Wait on the sign, before we get caught up in the streams of toil.

Staying up late burning the midnight oil is frying our focus and
        blocking our spiritual hearing.

When we slumber unencumbered, we will wake up with the freedom
        to move renewed in our strength.

Chorus:
Rest in the garden will renew your strength. Rest in the garden will
        renew your life.

Take a retreat from the chores, delegate the duty,
Sleep on a decision,
Catch up on your beauty rest on a constant basis.
Better yet, set up a cycle for optimal functioning.
Say a prayer when you wake up worrying.

Get you some sleep, girl. Lay down and rest.
The best parts of us are exhausted sometimes.
Close your eyes, take a nap and in this rest you will find that your
        mind absolutely needed that break to crack open the windows
        of your vision.
 Our intuition is working just fine, but we can't listen if our mind is
        bogged down.
Sometimes we need to get out of town or take a staycation.
Sit down for a spell; and the strategy for a new creation will come
        when the whole being is refreshed.
How can herstory write itself without perpetual rest?
How can you walk in your power and glory and remain limitless
        without rest?
Let us relinquish ourselves from all of this busy-ness and prioritize the
        business of getting some rest.

Chorus:
Rest in the garden will renew your strength. Rest in the garden will
renew your life.

Sacred Tongues

Are our tongues not sacred, so much so, that we have buried them in
the dirt with our forefathers wailing? Who am I to speak on her
skin? Red and hewn from Earth amber touched by terracotta.
She has found her worth in forming her heritage around the
sun. She speaks to me in a dialect akin to my own, but our
worlds are as similarly vast as the waters that separate our
ancestors.

She like me has birthed no ravens from her womb, but her hair is as
dark as onyx excavated at midnight.   The corners of her eyes
are tight and her lids are wrapped in coal.   She stole ancient
history from the scrolls of her upbringing and sang me a song of
destiny forgotten.

With lips soft as cotton she speaks the language that reminds me I am
so far removed from my Mother Land that the sands of my skin
can't recognize trade winds blown from the Ivory Coast. What I
yearn for the most is the connection to the roots stemming
upward of my family tree.

I yearn for her to see a little bit of herself when she looks at me.
Wish that I was not raised in ambiguity wilting in uncertainty.
Peeking through plantation quarters shrouded in mystery
stroking indistinguishable traits handed to me through genes
and homogenous origins that I can not see.

I am only knowledgeable of five generations that came before me. But
the palm of my outstretched hand can not summon or
command a grasp to comprehend who I really am. Never will I
know or understand the continent that continually circulates in

my veins. Won't recognize the correlation of tribal dance rhythms colliding in a pulsing strain of my hearts terrain.

I can not audibly claim alliance to any country within the continent from whence I know my people came. My words seem almost profane in my exchange with this woman who has spoken in the seed that gave birth to her speech. I do not envy but I admire as I ask her to teach me to say words so sacred I can not pronounce. Syllables so unfamiliar to my tongue and ear that the clarity of what I hear cannot translate to my lips. So I sip enlightenment from her and she curves her mouth in a dispensation of grace that evaporates the silence and paints this moment between us in purity. I sit and I sip until, I want to dig in the ground and search for a sound so holy.

That English becomes foreign to me and I speak and I speak sacredly.

ഐ സ്പീക്ക് സക്രെഡ്ലീ

Kiss Her

Kiss her, before love is forgotten.
For when eyes blink, love may unfold.
Keep your affections as close as lovers' hands doth hold.
Kiss her, before love is forgotten.
Before, love rotten, turns black and cold.
May your affections transmit with lips.
Kiss her, before love is forgotten.
For when eyes blink, love may unfold.

Make-out Haiku

#1
Your reservoir lips
the source of my hydration
I thirst for your kiss

#2
The moon will harvest
A sigh from your parted lips
Exhale, in my mouth

#3
We Fall into Spring
Our tongues balanced day and night
Perfect equinox

X & Y

I remember the X: I remember the Y
The connection of chromosomes, the sleight of hand
The magic tricks he used to slip past walls and peek around sharp
     corners.
You remember the moment the flame snuffed out in his eyes
How he stole the light from your soul.
The connection was lost, and his shoulder went cold.
You remember when lust turned languid, interest shifted like quick
     sand
The land beneath your feet was replaced by dead air.
You braced yourself for the impact of concrete.
Nothing could break the fall, your skin burst from the fracture and the
     cessation.
Days of silence followed.
Stillness wrapped itself around you like gauze.
Wounds cannot be sutured without words of healing,
so your pain was complete.

I remember the X: I remember the Y
The double helix of intersecting lives to form a complete.
You remember the immaterial substance how it festers into tangibility.
You saw the shadows take shape and begin their poltergeist play.
The overturning of truths like furniture strewn about by phantom
     tantrums.
You remember how your exodus was made light of by a callous
     hearted cut-off.
A Molotov explosion in the pit of your stomach rang out
The new miniature pyre you knew would never see the light of day,
Extinguished with anguish and two pills taken in succession.
Thus your agony was deafening.
I remember the X: I remember the Y

Code inlaid in a combination spiraling and unique,
You remember his imprint.
You recall the taciturn and neglectful posture of a man that wanted
    nothing to do with his offspring.
The bastion of hope was dashed by the disconnect.
You remember love situated just outside of your reach.
How unspoken passion postured itself dangling deformed in the air,
    oddly misshapen.
The replicating genes will do almost anything to survive in the wake of
    unfit circumstances.
Given your heart's condition you quickly adapted, mutating your
    strained emotions to remain alive.
You survived to carry the evidence of past life just as DNA.
Your truths are stored inside of me, the X and the Y.

For The Love Of 4 Names

It's like you've scattered your spirit across South Texas, touching all of us simultaneously. The seeds of your soul stirring words have found fertile earth and taken root over the years. Tears suffocate our skin, and we try to breathe in, blink away the thought of loss. We are watering your words with love and grief. Tonight, I am a weeping woman wishing upon every lone star in this state. I want the twinkle to return to your brown eyes. I want to resuscitate your lungs, amplify your voice, and reactivate your limbs. I cannot bring back the beautiful, bouncy, young, vibrant, Kellee 4 Names, that came into my world some six years ago and invigorated my life. I saw so much of myself in your hues. You colored my poetry with purpose. Gave the god in me a reason to stand up and speak. You crusaded a revival into my stanzas with your conviction. You were a walking collage of sparkling accessories, flouncy skirts, an incessant smile, and confidence. Wisdom never whispered around you. Wisdom was a clarion current. It surged through your very being arcing through your spine preventing your posture from ever slouching. Wisdom tumbled its' way through the creativity that manifested itself into your expressions. Wisdom was javelin triumphantly hurtling through your leadership, piercing its' way into our community. Lovely is the penetrating gaze of a thick haired brunette with cherubic cheeks bearing a prominent mole, a boot wearing sassy beauty queen, full of decadent laughter and graceful youth. Poise suited you well young poetess. Bravery boomed in every beat of your heart. Smart, head strong, curvy, as powerful throaty songs billowed from your body, as you pushed mountains aside to stride into your purpose. Every day you walked out your purpose. Challenged opposition and beat down every negative construct built against you. We were always with you, cheering you on. You have found your place, where you have always belonged, sweet angel. A paradise paved in gold greets you now. Somehow, we've got to learn to survive without your physical presence. All-America cowgirl, your essence has lassoed us. I am wrapped up in my memories stunned. How can you be gone; you were only 21? Young woman, from the first moment I heard you speak, at your very first slam at Ft. Sam 2009. I feasted on your lines, asked myself repeatedly, *Where did you come from?* You left us confounded by how you simply asked *how is this done?* You observed a few poets speak, then stepped to the mic like a seasoned pro. Letting light leak from your soul. You reach deep into our hearts, never letting us go. I still don't know how you picked up slam in approximately fifteen minutes. But I guess like everything else you do, you just put your passion in it. For the love of God, 4 Names, I cannot blame you for going home. BUT when I get there, I hope you've saved me a poem.

The Cost of a Protege Florence Price Poem

Virtuoso

Fingers dipped in satin
Sashaying and skimming across ivories and
Pleasing the tenderness of intonation
Melodies arrived
Uniquely across time, signature**, and** scale
And we await -
Breath baited hook, line, and sinker
In maritime
Afloat on salted ocean of sound

Composer

Bare knuckles braced against
Baby Grand
Index curled to the tip, pinky pointed to the ceiling
Gnarled bark branching out to the east and west
Limbs extended to embrace the breeze, like juniper trees
You bend
You hover
You bow
Beneath the music and uplift it

Woman

Life for you has been no crystal stair, yet you
Pulverized the obstacles
With symphonic composition
You didn't just take a seat at the table
You were standing in the orchestra pit and you let

Your very own concertos drift into the rafters
Let your sheets of notes stack to the ceiling
Gifted the chambers of the heart and throat with
The sweetest classical music
You wrote, and you wrote, and you wrote
And Sound awoke to serenade your heart with the dawning of apricot
colored day.

You wrote, and you wrote, and you wrote
And you played and you prayed
Psalms in brilliant billowing vibrato
And spoke spirituals in legato, no breath in between
Smooth and pristine
You let the petitions and the pain sing
God's praises in the palpitations of your heart
and the pulse of your palms
Pounding a profuse Fortissimo and tiptoeing along into silence
Morendo
Cornerstone of tempo
Protege of instrumentalists
 The universe swayed along
Measure by measure your harmonious waves
were dispensed in song.

You twinkle in the cosmos, in the throngs
with other heavenly beings.
Calm the morning with a litany of light.
Sketch vivid pastels for angelic voices to indwell.
So I acknowledge that it cost you everything,
Florence Price to prevail.
Now you are the revival,
the Renaissance for the universe of art to inhale.

Your compositions are regaled and hailed
With the grandeur they've always deserved.
Virtuoso,
Composer,
Woman

You are lauded with a legacy preserved.

Vampire

A vampire can't come inside until he is invited. SO you are saying I can't blame you Lost Boy. You crossed over the threshold and stole blood from the nape of my neck. Pecked hollowing holes and kept sucking me dry to the bitter end. Couldn't even call you boyfriend. You never did like titles. Preferring ambiguous charades, had me concealed in a coffin hiding from sun rays and the clarity that comes with luminous light. We could only be seen together in the cloak of night. I still fight to slay the demons you leave behind. Bats sway suspended lining my cave of a soul. I have no crucifix or garlic so feeble minded I fold. Hold tight to my holy water though, hoping to cleanse the places you defiled. If only I would have seen your ferocious fangs the first time you smiled. I mean, I was always taught to beware of wolves dressed like sheep. So on full moons I would count silver bullets to fall asleep. I guess in our case, denial is the counterpart of deception. I should have recognized the clues and drew the connection between the blood at the scene and the stake you vehemently drove through my heart. Ironically, you also played the part of Van Helsing as if my bounty was a vendetta... inventing new weapons so that I could be slain, and then you departed as quickly as you came. But I would rather call you Count Dracula than call you by your real name. I am so shamed by the fang marks impetuously imprinted in my skin. Still the seducing scent of sanguineous attraction draws me back in. I now thirst for blood from the primal hunting games you taught me so well. I am doomed to roam the earth alone, but it feels like a torrid and tortured hell. So I am a shell of skin... where a woman used to be. My tale will be immortalized for centuries to come, but will you remember me? Yes I pale from my lack of iron coupled with emotional anemia. I despise my deficiency. It's you who drew first blood and tasted the essence of who I used to be. The moon is calling, I need to drink. My body is weak from craving crimson in imminent urgency. These feelings curdle inside of me. My desire is bloody, baby, bittersweet. I am a vampire; and I need to drink. It seems I am just as lost as the boy who found me, and left me starving, thirsty for love.

Precious Jewel

I want to borrow words from Psalms and Proverbs to describe how love becomes sacred when unearthed from rock. Through lineage, through blood thicker than the water and clay that make up my skin and sinew. But the parts of us that will eternally continue are invisible and indestructible, not fragile, as our flesh. So I will press this precious jewel to my chest and move forward. This may sound like sorrow, but there is hope wrapped in this lament. For the years that I've spent picking up your mannerisms like smooth stones. I've gathered your stories into this bosom. They have ripened me to my bones. I have grown up loving this nurturing matriarch from the start to the finish. May your value increase, though your body diminished. The sound of your laughter left my spirit replenished. So I will press this precious Jewel to my chest and move forward. I have learned what it means to be concerned, from the way you weave an inquisitive rhapsody into the composition of your words. How your glittering eyes would telescope my constellations searching for obedience and honesty. *Everything is fine, Granny* became my automatic reply. How you would sigh from my lack of understanding, your sensibility and sensitivity demanding I take heed. Your thoughtfulness is expressed in word and in deed. For a woman who spent her lifetime working until her body would no longer allow. For a woman who loved her children strong and proud. For a woman who taught me to be a lady and let nothing go to waste. For a woman that could create comfort in any space. For a woman that would cook you southern soul with flavor and spice. For a woman that would fuss over you to make every wrong turn right. For without this woman I would not know life. You are a radiant jewel that I will forever hold to the light. I will press your precious memory to my chest and move forward.

The Opiate

Verse 1:
She sips lonely like it's freshly brewed
Never stirs in sugar cubes
Vapors rising from percolating emotions and steeping memories
She drinks this cup empty
friendliness seeping from her laugh lines
smile sinking into a steaming hot liquid of bitterness and wrinkles
her nose crinkles like soggy tea bags from the toil of trying...
trying to be kind, trying to unwind, trying to find segues for small talk
she just stalks around strained like sap. She wants to relax,
but she spews words haphazardly.
Her personality doesn't shine like it used to.
Thirstily she keeps sipping cup after cup of this bland brew.
Waiting for a robust flavor to bust through
With a desire to pour out like the spout of a boiling kettle,
but simply not remembering how to.

Verse 2:
He breathes despair like it's filtered shorts
Chokes on carcinogens at the thought of divorce
Dispersing ringlets of sorrow from puckered lips clouding the air with
       remorse
He wants to kiss the budded lips of his wife. He wishes she would
       interrupt with each puff, but strife has built into the silence
Life has knelt into the silence, nowadays that's the only thing that
       escapes her eyelids
No sparks strike with the matches that gather in the ash tray
He is running out of words to say, running out to buy yet another pack
to smoke away his breath. He fears and inhales nothing is left
With the last drag exhaled and the cigarette laid to rest
Cancerous path to his grave is paved in cherry embers and gray ashes.

Verse 3:
She bleeds love like it's fiercely cut.
Razor to the fragile flesh wrist dangling up.
Her arms drip out the bloodied sound her words will never speak.
She slashes to get in touch with reality,
but only feeling the fluid from her body leak.
Self-loathing crashes into her memories.
She weeps suicide like it's an idle prayer from her sacred eyes.
Hallelujahs dripping scarlet onto her naked thighs.
Sirens will wail in the distance,
But she will never cry.
Limbs juxtaposed like a marionette doll waving goodbye.

Verse 4:
He laughs lonely,
jokes freely cracked, scrambled and fried
His feathers are puffed with pride.
He clucks mouth agape, head titled back.
Like a hen hatching heavy chuckles
From an even heavier heart.
Finishes first impressions with a false start.
He's a roosters crowing irony and puns in everyone of his punch lines.
He pecks away at people with cynicism and insults
that leave his truths undefined.
Cold shoulders and snap judgments
polishes his humor refined.
Smearing yellow yolks he plays the dirty-dozens to pass the time.
You will always find him stepping on those same eggshells that blow
        up like land mines.

Venus, Upon Landing

Upon your landing
They will think of you a materialized figment
Scoff secretly snickering at your savagery.
They will shield their eyes from the monstrosity
Select the parts of you that disgust them most,
then discuss them most
Find themselves too fascinated to turn away.
They will describe your four lips in foreign tongues.
Think you enigma
Call you *orangutan, ape-like, gorilla* with pale pointed fingers,
Like Death gesturing the gateway to Sheol,
Like an accusatory congregation turned executioners
They will want to crucify your image
bleed you dry in their cross hairs
Coop your spirit, yet set your gyrating body free.
Your every movement will become their amusement,
and your misery.
You are too tribal for their rhythm.
Your body is lost in a drum.
They will ransom your spread thighs.
You are stretched beyond this atmosphere.
Your brown is too buttery.
It slides across their cuticles as they poke.
They want to stroke away your strength.
Strip your buttocks nude and behold the leagues of your depth.
They have dissected your limbs,
yet they cannot grasp your raw anatomy.
You are beyond their comprehension.
Your presence commands too much attention.
The sight of you burns holes in their psyche.
You are a crater in the memory, so massive.

Upon landing you caused a sonic boom.
Consumed all of their energy, like a black out.
They cannot concentrate.
In return they will devour your flesh in every way imaginable.
They hunger for your different.
You taste rich upon their palate, but you turn so rancid in the gullet.
They cannot digest you fully.
They will gag upon regurgitated remains.
Their throats will sizzle with acidic bile,
like a rumba comingled with all of your flavors.
As you are heaved up they slip curses into your skin.
Upon landing all that remains is a vomited beautiful.
A morbid freak show of your sacred body.

I Continue

She drank a bottle of bravery, and placed an itchy wig on her vacant
      scalp.
She took her meds one by one and cast her demons out.
She knows survival like it was tattooed on her arm in Auschwitz.
A serial number and an unsterilized needle digging degradation into
      her once budding epidermis.
She knows survival like radiation -- penetrating burning resonance
      into her fondest faintest memory of an unoccupied land.

Her teary eyes recite a soliloquy for suffering and her lungs cough a
      sonnet of sadness that rattle her chest down to the lymph nodes
      in her breasts. But she will not be a sanctuary of lamenting
      forever. Her silver chord is hastened to an anchor unmovable.
      Her heart is harbored in an indestructible bunker. Faith cannot
      be tainted when focus is intact. She knows the potency of
      concentration. How it can camp like genocide on a nation. She
      knows the power of focus. How it can strip a people bare of its'
      identity. Try to obliterate them from an entire society. She
      knows the mayhem of martyrdom and the mark it has left on
      history. But she is a survivor!

She witnessed them brandishing the symbolism of the swastika like a
      bent and broken form of pure hatred. An ashen horse rode the
      perimeters of her home town plucking life's cup from a parched
      people then pushing and prodding them into cattle cars in the
      dreary frost of winter. She never entered the gas chambers.

She stands seven decades later with fingers that shake like a
      tambourine fastening a soft pink ribbon to her rose printed
      blouse pocket. She hooks a golden Star of David pendant to her
      necklace and latches it around her collar.

She bares her purpose like a metal of honor. She has not forgotten. She has been this brave before, been this bald before. Her body is well acquainted with frailty. Her spirit has known poverty, but she is rich in hope. She is in remission coping with cancer. She knows the answer. There is no Final Solution. She has faced extinction before. She has seen how pane swept the floor after the Night of Broken Glass. She's had to deny her Jewish heritage when asked. Now she will never be stripped of her identity again. Nor will denials' shame shadow her elderly frame.

"They call me the survivor," she said. "I pick myself up, zip my boots up, and I continue."

Eurydice

That inquisitive nature suits you like a delicate armor, however
You question yourself more often than you should, brave little
       princess.
Be resolute. Never let that glimmer in your sepia eyes vanish.
You are the daughter that I will never have.
If I could, I would shield you
from poisonous vipers that bathe their bellies in the fertile earth.
I know you cannot take every step with caution.
Your carefree spirit will not allow this.
When the troubadours come wooing you with their tune,
choose a suitor with whom you resonate harmoniously.
Build upon that vibration, and together, shake the world.
You are more beautiful than my poetry can express, little girl.
Your image is immortalized in my mind.
When your personal Orpheus finds you
may the notes of his lute stroke your skin with admiration
for the radiant goddess you were born to be.
I will see you in the cosmos gleaming, like your smile has
Every time that I have beheld you, and called you by name,
       sweet Eurydice.

On the Eve of Yearning

Bid me to the forbidden
The hiss of your words a sanctuary for my desire.
Over the threshold of temptation I saunter
Feeling the cool of your wooing at my spine,
until I no longer hear the faint murmur of my conscience.
You have stalked me to the pulp.
Slithered down branches tethering reptilian scales to beautiful bark
gliding so close to truth that your resemblance melds chameleon like
        in essence.
You tell me of how sweet sampled nectar may taste on my budding
        curiosity,
so that I feel as though I have already partaken of this succulent
        wonder.
The weight of my fingers is desperate and heavy as they fumble
        towards the foliage.
You must have been an angel in another realm.
Your words fall like grace upon my earlobes.
Feathers of a whisper dance around my memory,
but those virtues are just beyond my reach now.
I will not surely die if I take just one delicate bite.
Paradise will be more sumptuous once my understanding has been
        exposed.
A visage of vastness awaits just beyond the vacuity of the present.
My hunger is barren.
My belly is void of flavor that I have no recollection of upon my palate.
I no longer savor the innocence of any other fruit.
The taste of unfamiliarity nags at the tip of my tongue urging me to
        indulge.
I bite down to the core and enamel hits knowledge as a new taste
        rushes over my senses.

Experience rinses over my tongue, escapes down to my chin, and falls
    on my flesh.
Yet, I yearn.

Amanda

She has a swollen belly
filled with promise.
Unharmonious hormones
are causing a commotion in her body.
Hoping for a miracle
when asked what she wants
Amanda's only reply is *a healthy baby*.
Her stomach hardens as sedimentary changes shape.
She flashes hot. She shivers cold
She craves.
Her body aches in every crevasse imaginable
still she perseveres.
Symptoms wax and wane like the moon that's
ever evolving in her abdomen.
She grows.
Her body a shape shifting canvas of colors and discomfort.
Despite it all I see the joy she is experiencing in the midst of pain.
It's amazing how a woman on birth control can end up pregnant
and still want her child. I admire her for this.
She has grown.

Maggie Lena Walker

About the Business

When they speak of you, Maggie, it will be more than a briefcase. Businesswoman. Philanthropist. Suffragist. They will speak of your power-suited prowess. Shower you in praise for the funds and families you raised up by the bootstraps. You successfully assisted the black people of Richmond establish ownership of hearth and home. Worth your weight in gold. Stories should be told of your grandeur. From laundry baskets and poverty to President of St. Luke's Penny Savings Bank. We have you to thank for crossing thresholds to boldly stand where prominent men have always stood. Made the most with your hands and auspiciously turned good sense into great dividends. You presided over the Independent Order of St. Luke until it consolidated with two other banks. We appreciate all you did to map out this blueprint. For your stewardship we salute you. You were a true reformer, a teacher, a mother, an entrepreneur who helped to build a city and lift a community on your very own back. Eliminating scarcity and lack with your mindset and business strategies. You were as boss as any lady could be and we see you and spread a spotlight across your name, Maggie Lena Walker. It takes a woman like you, being about her business, to change the game.

Your Name

Your named foamed up like a peroxide rinse
and gathered at the corners of my mouth.
Your name trickled to the surface and clotted on my skin forming a
    scab.
Your name seeped from my pores like sweat then ran profusely down
    my spine and began soaking my shirt.
Your name built up like bile in my stomach and lurched towards my
    esophagus.
Your name keeps meeting me unexpectedly at the intersections of
    every road I travel, so it's virtually unavoidable.
Your name has become a massive pothole on a one lane street and
    there is no sidewalk or median.
Your name cannot be sidestepped.
I have attempted to keep my distance from it.
When silence could no longer carry me over the speed bump of your
    name in conversation
I further tried to swerve past the confrontation of syllables.
The comfortability of the pronunciation used to feel like velvet on my
    lips.
 I was so used to slipping into your name like it was wool pajamas on a
    rainy day.
But the fibers of that fabric became itchy and
they caused too much friction on my frame that I cannot bear the burn
    marks nor the agitation any longer.
So I started sleeping stark naked, resting on my pillow trying not to
    conjure you in my sleep.
Trying not to mumble your name in my dreams. But who can control a
    dream?

Only the Sandman himself conducts the symphony of nightfall with
        foolish fantasy that mimics reality.
I awaken with the breath of morning.
no, literally morning breath, and attempt once again to rinse you out.

What Comes Before

Poetry before bedtime
Twilight before dawn
Beauty before brawn
Peace before storm
Queen before hive
Love before pride
Death before life
Ripening beyond the vine
A summons in every line
to tell a tale of unforsaken truths
With each pen stroke a plucking of forbidden fruit.

Overly Ripened: A Psalm of Lamentation

Verse 1:
When loose replaces taut. What serums can be bought for these under eye circles, puffs and bags? Here's the real gag,
collagen and estrogen used to be my closest friends. But then stretch marks & wrinkles decided to start beefing with me. My skin is hyperpigmented and the veins are showing, chin hair growing. I got these lumpy legs, everything is beginning to spread. Just look at this arm flab, back fat, and cellulite! My hairline ain't sitting right. My morning face could stir a fright. It's very scary, not contrary, or trite.

Chorus:
I remember when my fruit was supple and ripe for the picking. I recall before my biological clock started ticking and age started kicking my tail. Youth is a fleet of ships setting sail. Beauty is a fugitive. I'm in pursuit, but thrown off of the trail.

Verse 2:
When did my vision fail? I'm trying on fashionable readers to magnify the fine print. My time is spent researching skin care and hair treatment regimens to keep it clear, keep it full, keep it thick. Any color other than gray and white, take ya pick. Gotta stay equipped with bottled water and a portable fan, in case a hot flash hits dryland. This internal inferno doesn't skip a day. When my body overheats, I do not play. I don't jokes or make light. Not to mention my emotions are a stick of dynamite!!

Chorus:
I remember when my fruit was supple and ripe for the picking. I recall before my biological clock started ticking and age was kicking my tail. Youth is a fleet of ships setting sail. Beauty is a fugitive. I'm in pursuit, but thrown off of the trail.

Bridge:
I cannot say when it started, this uphill battle with going downhill. I wonder what menopause brings and how does it feel to be the eldest woman in the room? These branches need pruning for this aging fruit, before it all droops. Can I get to the root of my concerns before insecurity starts to burn a hole in my vision? Dear God, it's me Andrea, are you listening?

Verse 3:
The sag of it. The skin tags of it. I mean moles and crows feet... the deep seated unsightly flare ups of random things. IT is God awful the gifts that old age brings. I cannot sing of this inglorious sight. I need a lotion for the day and cream for the night. It's like being a vampire, avoiding the UV Rays of light. Who consumes this fruit that is overly ripe? I ask, perturbed. The answer is, Time. And he's a greedy bastard.

Uncaged

Poised and statuesque ready for flight
Rinsed in sultry indigo stage light
A queen spreads her wings and peacock struts to center stage
Patent leather stilettos peep toes
show Vamp nail lacquer adorned by rhinestones,
sequined skirt accented by a high slit to mid-thigh,
Satin shirt half buttoned
Revealing a raven colored push-up with red lace trim,
Single strand of pearls draped in the plunge,
Matte rouged lips,
Sterling silver piercing juts from a pointed beak grazing,
Bronzer contouring high definition cheek bones,
Kohl liner tracing the lids hovering above
Mascaraed lashes that bow with a swans' grace.
The music begins...
A neck cranes as a chiseled chin tilts to the sky.
Mouth agape silence escapes.
A pantomime of beauty tracing the lyrics of
A song unsung.
A fanfare of feathers spread the expanse of the heavens above
the sleek silhouette of this airborne bird before
A descent in flight begins.
The final muted notes peak as curtains draw to a close
Surmounted by thunderous applause.
A diva withdraws from the stage removing his wings
returning to the nest of manhood.

How Insensitive

Some things were made fragile, meant to be handled delicately. For instance, a wine goblet. Too much pressure applied to the stem and it will snap. Too much force administered to the rim and it will crack. Too tight a squeeze to the bowl and it will simply break.

I can no longer fake it. We falter when the stress point is reached. In the midst of all the celebration fingertips pressed firmly but the glass was too fine. Maybe the grapes spoiled on the vine. I can only evade. You receive this calculated stare whenever you open your mouth to speak. Past the moment and point of no return. Words are no longer revered. Because reverence is only reserved for the savory moments, when lust flows like libations. Liquid hands brushing across lips. Laughter is a flirtatious melisma that we make with our bodies. The language of a body will crystalize when chilled. We were swirling and swishing around like wine in glasses tilted in a toast. We clink too hard, collide and scar ourselves Oh so easily. Time is a textured folly. Abrasive, and we were made fragile. You seize this moment aggressively and say, "I love you." Once upon a time, I was thirsty for your love and your sensation pleased me.

Now you've become:

A burning at the back of the throat. A tingle in the middle of the mouth, like a concentrated fermentation, distilled spirit, heavy proof. Today, I sip it slowly, remain aloof, stony and removed from the moment. I wore no shades, but there was a definite haze of smoke covering my irises and pupils. No glinting fire. No embers burning, the kindling snuffed out. We play the hand we are dealt. Poker faced. No bluff, no trump, just cut throat. As you spoke, I emptied my glass and then wiped my mouth of the situation.

I exit into the bustle of traffic. Horns blaring, I escape to the rhythmic click of pedestrians striding through the crosswalk. Flashes of yellow allude to the yielding of the situation. Before the flare of red.

All good things come to an end. I can still hear your voice echoing, "I love you," in my head. I have fled the scene absconding, as a callous hearted fugitive.

I guess you will always remember me as selfish and insensitive. But some things were made fragile and inevitably hearts will be broken.

My Funny Valentine

Humor me with a love so sultry.
I will giggle from the sugar-coated sentimental moments beside you.
Tickle me with an intimate kinetic possibility.
Sparks flying jokingly around, even though I've always considered love
      to be serious business.
You've decorated this meeting like a clown, managed to turn my mood
      right-side up from upside-down before presenting me with
      hugs
covered in dark chocolate hearts.
Boxed in small compartments.
I'm swooning for your smirky lips.
I'm seduced by your slapstick.
Hands quick to draw me in close like a heart hypnosis. Swinging on a
      pendulum pulled and swayed into the moment as your audience
      of one.
I'm laser focused on the comedy, coddling the neck of our romance,
      dining on the candor of your banter such a delicious
      lighthearted laughter.
Always looking for ways to enhance the punchline.
So that I may lavishly smile for the longest time.
My Funny Valentine.
My sweet comic, Valentine.

The Fall

Cotton candy tapestry,
taffeta bows and cushy throw pillows became my place of landing.
A serenade of softness surrounded my feet.
I was lifted then
I was planted firmly in bountiful affection. I followed the direction of
  zooming arrows to the sight
of Eros.
I tiptoed and traipsed to romantic tunes,
until my knees buckled from the beauty.
Electric clouds let loose a cascade of desire descending upon me.
My soul was saturated.
I felt appreciated.
My toes were glitter polished in poetry.
Twinkling and shiny rays danced off of my skin, warm as the heavens
All of this to say, it was absurdly sweet the way your love knocked me
  off my feet.
I heard Stevie Wonder and Sinatra singing.
Tender troubadour harmonies unfolded around me. My hopes began
  to hum along to the honied ballads of song.
 I was embraced by salutations ringing in chorus.
The birds chirped a little louder. Rainbows arched higher overhead
  vibrantly. Color after color spoke charmingly.
Feathery fuchsia sensations and smoked purple passion
tinted the scenery, sashaying in zigzags and whimsical streaks.
My heart found its peak
and I have tipped
 over.

Acknowledgments

2024 -"Sacred Tongues"
Poem published in Torch Literary Arts, August 2024 Feature

2025 - "The Body as Religion" in *Formidable Woman* at
http://formidablewoman.org/?p=72413 published by D. Ellis Phelps

About the Author

Andrea "Vocab" Sanderson is a San Antonio native, and the city's 1st African American Poet Laureate Emeritus serving a term from 2020 to 2023. After retiring from a twenty year career with Bexar County Juvenile Detention Center, she took on a new career as the Arts Education Coordinator for the Carver Community Cultural Center. Vocab has facilitated creative writing and performance workshops and featured with her poetry and music internationally from conferences to university teaching residencies. Some of her awards include: *Courageous Love Award* by the First Universalist Unitarian Church 2024. *Literary Excellence Award* by Gemini Ink 2024. The Arts and Letters Award in 2020 by friends of San Antonio Public Library. Best Literary Advocate by San Antonio Magazine, in 2020. She was voted Best Local Poet in: 2024, 2023, and 2021 by the San Antonio Current.

In 2021, she received an Academy of American Poets Laureate Fellowship for her intergenerational oral history initiative, *The Echo Project*.

Vocab's commissioned poetry and voice are featured in several commercials and documentaries. She's had the distinct honor of opening up for the late great Nikki Giovanni, Dr. Cornel West, and Phylicia Rashad. She was recently awarded a Creative Development Grant by National Performance Network, for her collaboration concert with Lubana Al-Quntar that was commissioned by The Carver and Art 2 Action. This theatrical concert debuted at The Carver on May 3, 2024 and is entitled, "*The Seasoned Woman,*" with plans to tour the U.S. in 2025 and 2026.

Vocab's debut book is entitled: *She Lives In Music*, published by *Flower Song Press*. Her latest book, *The Seasoned Woman, is available on Gnashing Teeth Publishing;* March 2025. Stream her poetry and music on all major streaming platforms.

Visit her website to find out more at: www.andreavocabsanderson.com

www.ingramcontent.com/pod-product-compliance
Lightning Source LLC
Chambersburg PA
CBHW051333120626
46547CB00016B/2524